COLORING PLUS ACTIVITIES

Heroes of the Bible

Publisher	Arthur L. Miley
Vice President & Editor	Carolyn Passig Jensen
Art Director	Debbie Birch
Cover Design	Gary Zupkas
Production Director	Barbara Bucher
Production Assistant	Valerie Fetrow
Assistant Editor	Janet Ackelson
Illustrator	Ann Morton
Production Artist	Nelson Beltran
Proofreader	Barbara Bucher

Copyright © 1995 • Sixth Printing
Rainbow Books • P.O. Box 261129 • San Diego, CA 92196

#RB37163
ISBN 0-937282-47-2

COLORING PLUS ACTIVITIES
Heroes of the Bible

How to Use This Book

These reproducible coloring activities are designed to teach young children biblical principles and stories, and help them apply these important Bible truths to their own lives in practical ways.

These activities are designed to be used in the classroom under the direction of a teacher or leader; they are ideal for Sunday schools, children's church, Vacation Bible Schools, Wednesday night "kid's clubs", and Christian schools.

These coloring activity sheets bring new fun and variety to Bible learning. They are designed to supplement and reinforce Bible stories or lessons or around which to build class sessions. Every activity is created especially for the interests and learning abilities of children ages 4 to 8 years. This book is one of eight similar books which cover many basic, foundational Bible teachings.

This book contains 48 delightful coloring and activity sheets, plus teaching tips and ideas for teachers on how to use the coloring and activity sheets to teach important biblical concepts. All sheets may be reproduced for use with children in Bible-teaching classes.

The coloring and activity sheets in this book are grouped into four thematic chapters. Each chapter begins with two pages of teaching tips which provide the teacher with helpful hints for lesson ideas, instructions for using the coloring and activity sheets, directed conversation to help teach biblical concepts, and much more. (Directed conversation is printed in boldface.) The teaching tips help the teacher relate the spiritual lessons to the children's lives in practical ways they will understand.

Each of the coloring and activity pages in this book includes a picture to color and memory verse on the front side of the sheet. A related activity and another memory verse which teach the children to apply God's Word to their lives, are on the other side of the sheet. Activities include mazes, pictures to color, connect-the-dots, find-and-circle exercises, and much more.

The teacher may chose to reproduce both the coloring sheet *and* the activity sheet, or use either the coloring sheet *or* the activity sheet in one class session. (For most effective learning, however, a copy of both the coloring sheet *and* the corresponding activity sheet should be made for each student.)

First talk with the children about the picture to color, read the caption and teach the memory verse using the teaching tips for the coloring sheet found at the beginning of the chapter. When the children have completed coloring the picture, talk about the corresponding activity sheet, read the caption, teach the memory verse, and guide the children in doing the activity, again using the teaching tips at the beginning of the chapter as your guide. As you work with the children, be sure to relate the biblical lesson to the lives of the children.

The children should also be encouraged to take their coloring and activity sheets home, tell their family what they learned and display the sheets to help them remember the practical application of the lesson. Memory verses may be reviewed in later classes to assure the children really do make the Bible lessons these sheets teach part of their lives.

Crayons or felt-tip markers are all that are required for most activities. Pencils, scissors, construction paper and glue, paste or tape may be used occasionally. The pages in this book are perforated for easy removal of the sheets for copying.

The New King James Version is the biblical reference used through this book, unless noted otherwise.

These coloring activities make it easy to teach important biblical concepts in practical ways children understand and remember.

CONTENTS

Old Testament Heroes

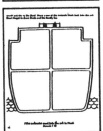

Noah
Pages 9 and 10

Read or tell the Bible story from Genesis 6:13-9:17.

Coloring Sheet: Help the children color the bands of the rainbow in various bright colors. Talk about how the earth must have been after the flood. Then learn the memory verse. Ask each child to name one thing in the earth which belongs to God. If desired, the children could do this in sentence prayers, saying, "Thank you, God for grass." "Thank you, God for clouds." "Thank you, God for animals," etc.

Activity Sheet: Talk to the children about the special things Noah had to do to care for the various animals on the ark. Then direct the children to draw animals in three of the spaces in the ark and to draw Noah and his family in the fourth space. Help the children learn the memory verse. If desired, the children could review the verse by saying, "The elephants went into the ark to Noah." "The giraffes went into the ark to Noah." "The horses went into the ark to Noah," etc.

Abraham
Pages 11 and 12

Read or tell the Bible story from Genesis 17:1-8, 16-21; 21:1-7.

Coloring Sheet: Talk about how Abraham and Sarah must have felt when Isaac was born. Say, **God kept His promise to Abraham that he and Sarah would have a baby. God keeps His promises to us too.** Talk about some of God's promises to us. Ask, **Has God kept this promise?** Introduce the memory verse by saying, **The Bible says God keeps His promises. Learn the verse together.**

Activity Sheet: Read or tell the Bible story from Genesis 22:1-13. Say, **God wanted to see how much Abraham believed and trusted in Him. God saw that Abraham trusted Him completed. We should trust God completely too.** Read the photo caption aloud. Assist the children in finding and coloring the sheep and in finding and circling the seven things which should not be in the picture. Then say, God provided a lamb for Abraham. God will also provide things we need. Learn the memory verse together.

Moses
Pages 13 and 14

Read or tell the Bible story from Exodus 3:1-10; 14:1-31.

Coloring Sheet: Read the picture caption to the children. Talk about the picture, pointing out the water on either side of the people crossing the Red Sea. Say, **Our memory verse says God is present to help in trouble. God protected His people from the cruel king. God can protect and help us when we are in trouble too.** Help the children to think of times the Lord can help them. Learn the Bible verse together.

Activity Sheet: Talk about the way the Israelites traveled to the Promised Land. Talk about each of the pictures and help the children circle in blue the modern-day transportations and circle in red the ways God's people traveled. Then say, **God is with us no matter where we go.** Ask the children to name places they could go (other towns, states, countries, etc.) Ask, **Would God be with you in Africa? Would God be with you in Chicago?** Learn the verse together.

Gideon
Page 15 and 16

Read or tell the Bible story from Judges 6:11-16; 7:1-25.

Coloring Sheet: Ask the children to point out in the picture the three things Gideon and his army used to defeat the Midianites (torch, pitcher and trumpet). Then say, **Gideon was afraid, but God was with him to help him. Sometimes we are afraid too, but God is with us too.** In learning the memory verse, let the children think of times they might be afraid and say the verse this way: "The Lord is my helper: I will not fear when I have a test in school." "The Lord is my helper; I will not fear when it is dark and stormy at night," etc.

Activity Sheet: Talk again about how the men for Gideon's army were selected and help the children choose which men would be in Gideon's army and which would not. Ask, **Which way would you drink?** Then say, **God promises He is with us and will watch over us. God was with Gideon and His army and they defeated the enemy. God is with us and will help us too.** Learn the memory verse together.

Daniel
Pages 17 and 18

Read or tell the Bible story from Daniel 6.

Coloring Sheet: Ask the children, **If you knew you might be hurt or die because you obeyed God, what would you do? Daniel obeyed God no matter what and God protected him.** Tell about modern-day persecutions of Christians. Say, **It is not easy to obey God when you know you might be hurt or killed, but God will help us trust and obey Him no matter what.** Learn the memory verse.

Activity Sheet: Read the picture caption and discuss the question together. Then direct the children to connect the dots to show a child praying. Ask, **What should you do when people are mean to you? What did Daniel do?** Introduce and learn the memory verse. Talk about prayer. Be sure the children understand that prayer is talking to God and that they can pray to God and tell Him anything at anytime and from anyplace. Ask, **What does our memory verse say God will do when we pray to Him?** Close the class with each child praying a short sentence prayer.

Jonah
Pages 19 and 20

Read or tell the Bible story from Jonah 1-3.

Coloring Sheet: Read the picture caption to the children. Talk about what it might have been like inside the stomach of the big fish. Then say, **It would have been better if Jonah had obeyed God the first time. What should we do when we know God wants us to do something?** After the children have answered, say, **We ought to obey God. That is our memory verse for today.** Then ask the children to name times when they should obey God. After a child names a situation, the whole class may say, "We ought to obey God" until the verse is memorized.

Activity Sheet: Review the events of the story of Jonah as the children complete the maze. Say, **If Jonah had obeyed God the first time, he wouldn't have gotten into trouble. We should always obey God.** Learn the memory verse together.

Noah

God told Noah to build a big boat, called an ark, to protect his family and every kind of animal from a great flood. After the flood, God made a rainbow and promised He would not destroy all living things by a flood again.

The earth is the LORD'S, and everything in it

Psalm 24:1 NIV

God told Noah to take two or more of every kind of animal into the ark so they would not die in the flood. Draw some of the animals Noah took into the ark. Don't forget to draw Noah and his family too.

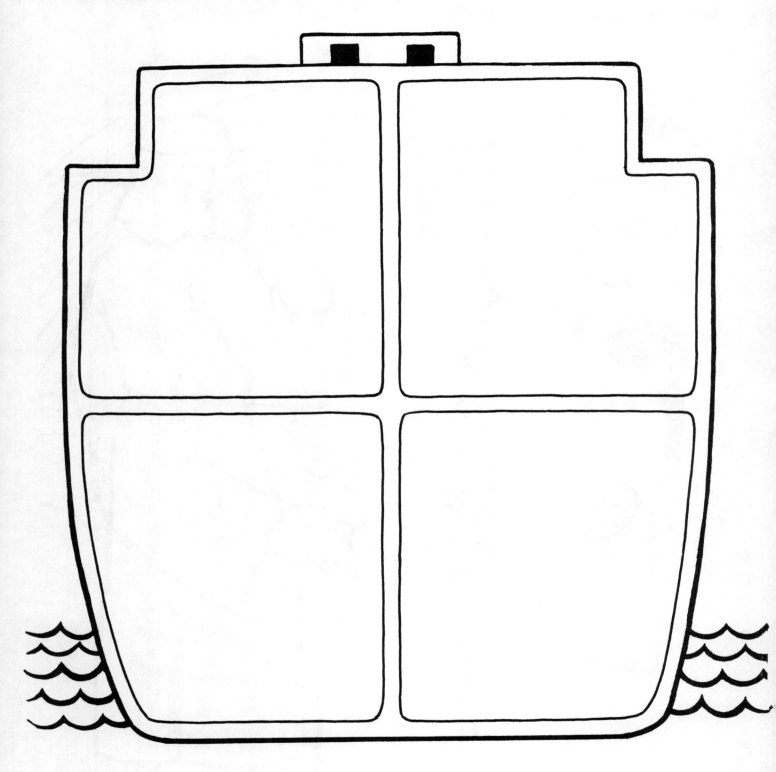

(The animals) went into the ark to Noah
Genesis 7:15

Abraham

Abraham and his wife Sarah were too old to have children, but God promised they would have a son and many grandchildren. When Abraham was 100 years old, Isaac was born. This teaches us God keeps His promises to us.

He who promised is faithful.
Hebrews 10:23

God told Abraham to take Isaac and go worship God. God told Abraham there was a sheep caught in a bush which Abraham was to sacrifice to the Lord. Find and color the sheep hidden in this picture. Find and circle seven other things which should not be in the picture.

God will provide . . . the lamb
Genesis 22:8

Moses

God asked Moses to lead God's people out of Egypt away from the cruel king. When they came to the Red Sea, God made the sea become dry land so His people could cross safely. This story teaches us that God will protect His people.

God is . . . a very present help in trouble
Psalm 46:1

Moses and God's people traveled for many years to get to the new land God promised them. Put a red circle around the ways God's people traveled to the Promised Land. Put a blue circle around the ways you could travel if you were going to live in a new place.

I am with you . . . wherever you go
Genesis 28:15 NIV

Gideon

God asked Gideon to lead God's people into battle. Gideon was afraid, but he did what God asked. God gave Gideon and his army great victory. This story teaches us to obey God even when we are afraid.

The LORD is my helper; I will not fear.
Hebrews 13:6

God told Gideon how to choose the men to be in his army. The men who stood and used their hands to drink were to be in the army. The ones who knelt down to drink were sent home. Circle all the men who would be in Gideon's army. Cross out the men who would not be selected.

I am with you and will watch over you
Genesis 28:15 NIV

Daniel

Some bad men wanted to kill Daniel, so they put him into a den of lions because he prayed to God. God protected Daniel and the lions did not hurt him. This story teaches us that when we do right, God will protect us.

Whoever trusts in the Lord shall be safe
Proverbs 29:25

Sometimes people try to hurt other people because they believe in God. Has anyone ever done something mean to you because you believe in Jesus? Connect the dots to show what you should do when this happens. Daniel did this too.

I will call on You, O God, for You will answer me
Psalm 17:6 NIV

Jonah

Jonah did not want to do what God told him to do, so God made a big fish swallow Jonah. After Jonah repented, the fish spit Jonah out, and Jonah did what God asked. This story teaches us to always obey God.

We ought to obey God
Acts 5:29

When God asks us to do something, we should always obey Him right away, not run away like Jonah did. Solve the maze to help Jonah find the way from his home to Nineveh to preach.

Nineveh

Do what is right and good in the sight of the LORD
Deuteronomy 6:18

New Testament Heroes

Peter
Pages 23 and 24

Read or tell the Bible story from Matthew 4:18-20 and Acts 2:14-47.

Coloring Sheet: Talk about Peter's life and service to the Lord. Discuss ways Peter told people about Jesus. Then talk about ways we can share God's love with others. Learn the memory verse together. Say, **God tells us in the Bible to tell other people about Him like Peter did. That's what it means to "preach the Gospel." We can do this wherever we are.** Talk about practical ways the children can tell others about Jesus.

Activity Sheet: Help the children understand that our actions are one way people know we love Jesus and are trying to live for Him. Instruct the children to look at each picture and decide if that activity shows people they love Jesus. The children may circle the actions which are pleasing to Jesus and cross out the others. Help them choose and color the picture showing a way they will share Jesus' love this week. Learn the memory verse, emphasizing that the children can set an example of Jesus' love no matter how young they are.

Nicodemus
Pages 25 and 26

Read or tell the Bible story from John 3:1-21. Use this story to present the plan of salvation to the children, using John 3:16 as the basis.

Coloring Sheet: Help the children understand that God sent Jesus to earth to die and come to life again so we can be forgiven from our sins and go to live in heaven forever. Learn the memory verse together. Then offer an opportunity for the children to accept Jesus as their Savior.

Activity Sheet: Talk about heaven and how wonderful it will be. Say, **Jesus has prepared a very special place where we can live forever if we believe in Jesus and have accepted Him as our Savior.** Learn the memory verse together, reiterating again the plan of salvation. Ask, **How do you feel when you think about living in heaven with Jesus?** Direct the children to draw their picture next to Jesus.

Zacchaeus
Pages 27 and 28

Read or tell the Bible story from Luke 19:1-10.

Coloring Sheet: Talk about sin and what it is. Say, **Sin is doing things which make Jesus sad.** Let the children name some sins. Then ask, **Have you ever sinned?** Show the children Romans 3:23 marked in your Bible. Say, **The Bible says all people have sinned, but our memory verse says that Jesus is ready to forgive us for our sins.** Show the children the memory verse marked in your Bible also. Learn the verse together and offer the children a chance to ask Jesus to forgive their sins.

Activity Sheet: Read the picture caption to the children. Then talk about each picture. Help the children decide and indicate if the actions shown are right or wrong. Say, **The Bible says if we confess our sins or tell Jesus we are sorry for the wrong things we've done, He will forgive our sins.** Learn the verse together. Then lead a prayer the children can repeat after you asking Jesus to forgive them for their sins.

Stephen
Pages 29 and 30

Tell the story of Stephen from Acts 6:1-7:60.

Coloring Sheet: Ask the children, **If you knew you might be hurt or die because you told about Jesus, what would you do? Stephen told about Jesus even though some bad men were going to kill him. He knew that if he died, he would go to heaven to live with Jesus.** Talk about modern-day persecutions of Christians. Then say, **It is not easy to tell about Jesus when you know you might be hurt or killed, but God is with us and nothing anybody can do can separate us from God.** Learn the memory verse.

Activity Sheet: Read the picture caption to the children and direct them to connect the dots to show a child praying. Ask, **What should you do when people are mean to you? What did Stephen do?** Introduce and learn the memory verse. Say, **What does the Bible say we should do when we have trouble?** Emphasize to the children that they can talk to God in prayer anytime and about anything. Let each child who wants to pray a short sentence prayer.

Paul
Pages 31 and 32

Read or tell the story of Paul's conversion from Acts 9:1-9.

Coloring Sheet: Talk about the picture. Point out the beam of light from heaven. Say, **Jesus had gone back to heaven, but He spoke to Paul, even though Paul couldn't see Jesus. A bright light shone down on Paul from heaven.** As you talk about Paul's missionary adventures, learn the memory verse, explaining what it means to speak boldly about Jesus. Suggest ways the children can tell about Jesus too.

Activity Sheet: Use the pictures to tell (or review) Paul's many missionary adventures. (This may be done over several class sessions.) Talk about ways the children can tell about Jesus wherever they go just like Paul did. Introduce the memory verse. Then say, **Paul went everywhere preaching the Word. You can too.** Then instruct the children to fill in their name and each say the verse in turn: "Jason went everywhere preaching the Word." "Cindee went everywhere preaching the Word," etc.

John
Pages 33 and 34

Read or tell about John's call to be Jesus' disciple in John 4:21-22. Show the children the book of John in the New Testament and Revelation 1:1 as proof of John's authorship of parts of the Bible.

Coloring Sheet: Talk about how the Bible was written. Point out the picture showing John carefully writing by hand. Say, **The Bible is God's special message to us. It tells us about Jesus and how we should live for Him.** Introduce and learn the memory verse. Say, **Who does the memory verse say Jesus is?** Talk about why it is important that we study the Bible to learn about Jesus.

Activity Sheet: Show the children the memory verse marked in your Bible. Then say, **The Bible is called the Scriptures. The Scriptures tell or testify about Jesus. What are some of the things the Bible tells us about Jesus?** Let the children cite stories about Jesus. If desired, you could have some stories pre-marked in your Bible to show and discuss. Learn the memory verse together. Then direct the children in finding and circling the hidden Bibles.

Peter

Peter **was one** of Jesus' disciples. He was a fisherman, but after Jesus went back to heaven, Peter became a great preacher and told many people about Jesus.

Go into all the world and preach the gospel
Mark 16:15

Peter loved Jesus very much. He told many people about Jesus. You can tell others about Jesus too. Circle the pictures showing ways you can show the love of Jesus to others. Then color one picture showing how you will share the love of Jesus this week. Cross out the pictures showing wrong or sinful actions.

Don't let anyone look down on you because you are young,
but set an example
1 Timothy 4:12 NIV

Nicodemus

Nicodemus was a very important leader. He came to talk to Jesus late at night because he wanted to learn more about Jesus. Later he told other people he believed in Jesus too.

He who believes in the Son has everlasting life
John 3:36

When we ask Jesus to forgive us for our sins and be our Savior, He will! We can go to be with Jesus in heaven someday. Draw a picture of yourself in the space below. Show how you feel when you know your sins are forgiven and you can live in heaven with Jesus.

Whoever believes in Him should not perish but have eternal life.
John 3:15

Zacchaeus

Zacchaeus came to hear Jesus preach. When he climbed up in a tree he could see. He told Jesus he was sorry for the wrong things he had done, and Jesus forgave him.

You, Lord, are good, and ready to forgive
Psalm 86:5

27

Zacchaeus was sorry for the wrong things he had done. Jesus forgave Zacchaeus. Jesus will forgive us too when we are sorry we did wrong. Circle the actions which please Jesus. Put an X on the things we should ask Jesus to forgive us for doing.

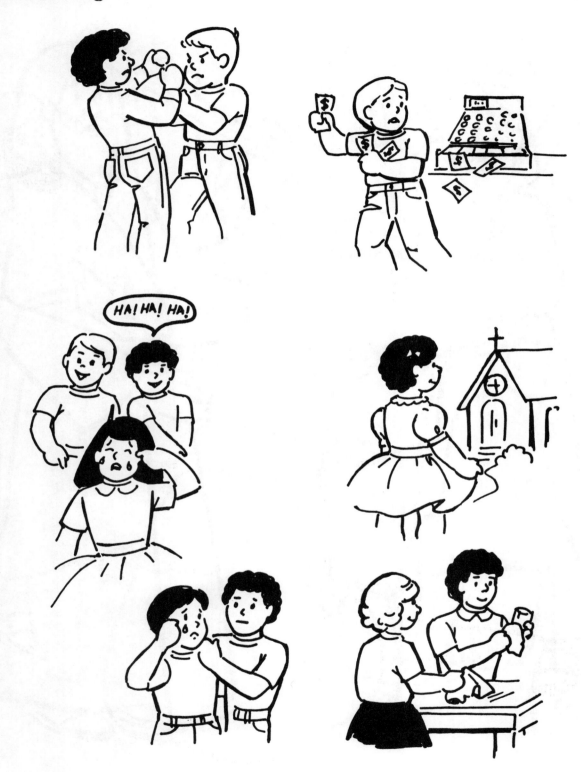

If we confess our sins, He is faithful . . . to forgive us our sins
1 John 1:9

Stephen

Stephen was one of the first Christians. He was very kind and helpful to others. He was not afraid to tell about Jesus, even though people were cruel to him because he was a Christian.

I will not fear. What can man do to me?
Hebrews 13:6

Stephen lived for Jesus and knew God would take care of him no matter what men did to him. God will take care of us and help us in hard times too. Connect the dots to see what you should do when you have problems. This is what Stephen did too.

Call upon Me in the day of trouble
Psalm 50:15

Paul

Paul used to hate the Christians who loved Jesus, but after he met Jesus on the road to Damascus, Paul became a great missionary. He traveled many miles to tell people about Jesus.

(Paul) spoke boldly in the name of the Lord Jesus
Acts 9:29

God led Paul to teach many people about Jesus in different countries. Even though Paul had many hard times because he was a Christian, he still obeyed and loved Jesus. Follow this path of Paul's life to see some of the things that happened to him. Color Paul in each picture. You can be a missionary like Paul by telling others about Jesus too.

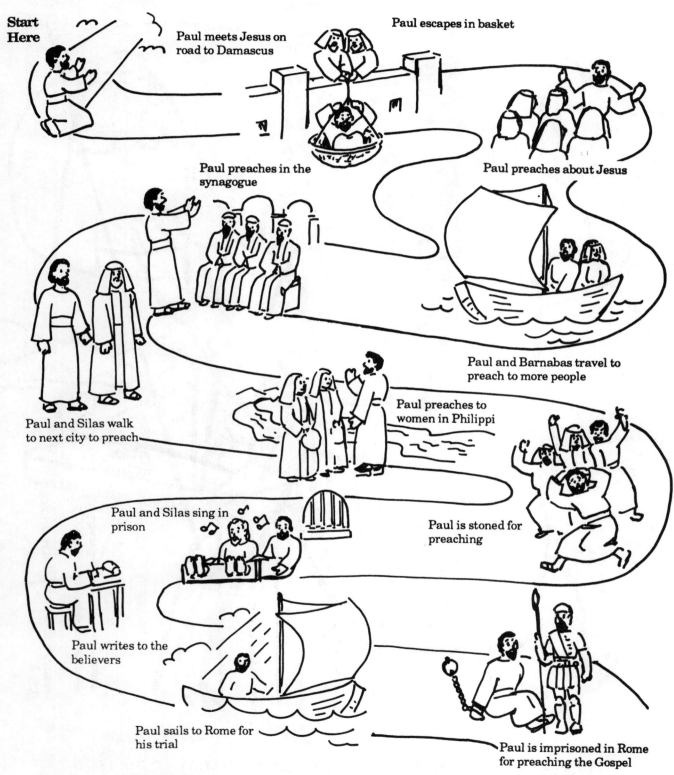

Start Here

Paul meets Jesus on road to Damascus

Paul escapes in basket

Paul preaches in the synagogue

Paul preaches about Jesus

Paul and Silas walk to next city to preach

Paul and Barnabas travel to preach to more people

Paul preaches to women in Philippi

Paul and Silas sing in prison

Paul is stoned for preaching

Paul writes to the believers

Paul sails to Rome for his trial

Paul is imprisoned in Rome for preaching the Gospel

(They) went everywhere preaching the word.
Acts 8:4

John

John was one of Jesus' very special disciples. John wrote part of the Bible which tells us about Jesus' life and miracles while He was on earth.

These are written that you may believe that Jesus is . . .
the Son of God
John 20:31 NIV

Our Bible tells about Jesus, God's Son and our Savior. There are seven Bibles hidden in the picture. Can you find and circle them all?

Scriptures . . . testify about (Jesus)
John 5:39 NIV

Bible Women

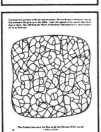

Sarah
Pages 37 and 38

Read or tell the Bible story from Genesis 17:1-8, 16-21; 21:1-7.

Coloring Sheet: Talk about how happy Sarah must have been when Isaac was born. If any of the children have a new baby at home, you may wish to talk about the happiness a baby brings. Say, **God kept His promise to Abraham and Sarah that they would have a baby. God keeps His promises to us too.** Talk about some of God's promises to us. Ask, **Has God kept this promise?** Then say, **God wants us to believe He will keep His promises.** Learn the memory verse together.

Activity Sheet: Say, **A long time before Jesus was born, God promised that He would send His Son to earth to save us from our sins. God kept His promise and Jesus was born.** Learn the memory verse together as a class and explain the plan of salvation. Offer an opportunity for the children to respond. Direct the children to color the dotted spaces to find the name JESUS.

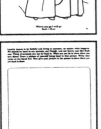

Ruth and Naomi
Pages 39 and 40

Read or tell the Bible story from Ruth 1-4.

Coloring Sheet: Define loyalty for the children. Then cite some situations which show loyalty and some which show disloyalty. Ask the children to distinguish between the two behaviors. Introduce the memory verse by saying, **God wants us to be loyal and faithful to each other, just like Ruth was to Naomi. One way we show our loyalty is by wanting to be with someone. Ruth wanted to go wherever Naomi went.**

Activity Sheet: Say, **God wants us to be loyal and loving all the time.** Learn the memory verse. Then help each child think of someone to whom they can be faithful and loyal. Discuss ways they can show their loyalty and love for that person and direct them in drawing a picture showing this. Help each child write his or her name on the line. The children should take their pictures home to give to the person they chose.

The Widow who gave
Pages 41 and 42

Read or tell the Bible story from 1 Kings 17:8-16.

Coloring Sheet: Ask the class, **What would you do if you only had a little bit of food, but you knew someone else needed it? Would you give it to them?** Talk about the Bible story, then say, **The Bible says if we give to people who are in need, God will provide for our needs.** Learn the memory verse together.

Activity Sheet: Read the picture caption to the children. Talk about each item in the room in turn and direct the children to circle the items which they would give to someone else who needed it. Say, **When we give something to someone who needs it, we are making Jesus happy. The Bible says God loves a cheerful giver.** Learn the verse together.

Esther
Pages 43 and 44

Tell the Bible story from Esther 1-10.

Coloring Sheet: Ask the children to tell what they would do if they knew someone was in trouble, but if they told about it, they might be hurt or killed themselves. Then say, **That is what happened to Esther. But Esther was brave. She knew it was more important to help someone else than to worry about what would happen to her.** Introduce the memory verse. Say, **The Bible says God is our helper when we have trouble. God helped Esther and God will help us too.**

Activity Sheet: Introduce the memory verse by saying, **God wants us to trust in Him whenever we are afraid. We can say, "Whenever I am afraid, I will trust in You."** Discuss each of the pictures as a class. Let the children tell how they would feel in each situation. After each, ask, **What should you do when you are afraid?** The children may answer with the memory verse, "Whenever I am afraid, I will trust in You."

Mary and Martha
Pages 45 and 46

Read or tell the Bible story from Luke 10:38-42.

Coloring Sheet: Look at the picture together. Ask, **Which one is Mary? What is she doing? Which one is Martha? What is she doing? Which one did Jesus say was doing the right thing? Why?** Talk with the children about what it means to "seek first the kingdom of God," and learn the verse. Say, **Jesus wants us to put Him first before our fun and work. He wants to be the most important thing in our lives.** Ask the class to join you in praying, **Dear Jesus, We want You to be the most important thing in our lives. Please help us to do what You want us to do all the time. In Jesus' Name. Amen.**

Activity Sheet: Look at each set of pictures and talk about which picture shows a child who is putting Jesus first in their lives. Say, **The Bible tells us to love the Lord with all our hearts. We show Jesus we love Him by putting Him first in our lives.** Learn the memory verse together.

Dorcas
Pages 47 and 48

Read or tell the Bible story from Acts 9:36-42.

Coloring Sheet: Say, **God has power over everything. God can make sick people well and people who have died come alive again.** Then say, **God made Dorcas come back to life to show the people His power. Many people believed in Jesus because Dorcas came back to life.** Then talk about the helpful things Dorcas did for others and learn the memory verse. Say, **After Dorcas came back to life, she helped many more people.**

Activity Sheet: Learn the memory verse first, then discuss each of the pictures in the left column and help the children draw a line to the picture in the right column which shows how they can be helpful in each situation. Talk about other situations in which the children can be kind and helpful to others as a way of showing God's love to them. Help each child think of one way they will be kind and helpful this week.

Sarah

Sarah was Abraham's wife. Even though she was too old to have a baby, God promised she and Abraham would have a baby. When Sarah was about 90 years old baby Isaac was born.

All things are possible to him who believes.
Mark 9:23

God kept His promise to Sarah and Abraham. We can be sure God always keeps His promises He gave us in the Bible. Color the spaces in the puzzle that have dots in them. You will find the Name of Someone God promised to send to save all of us from sin.

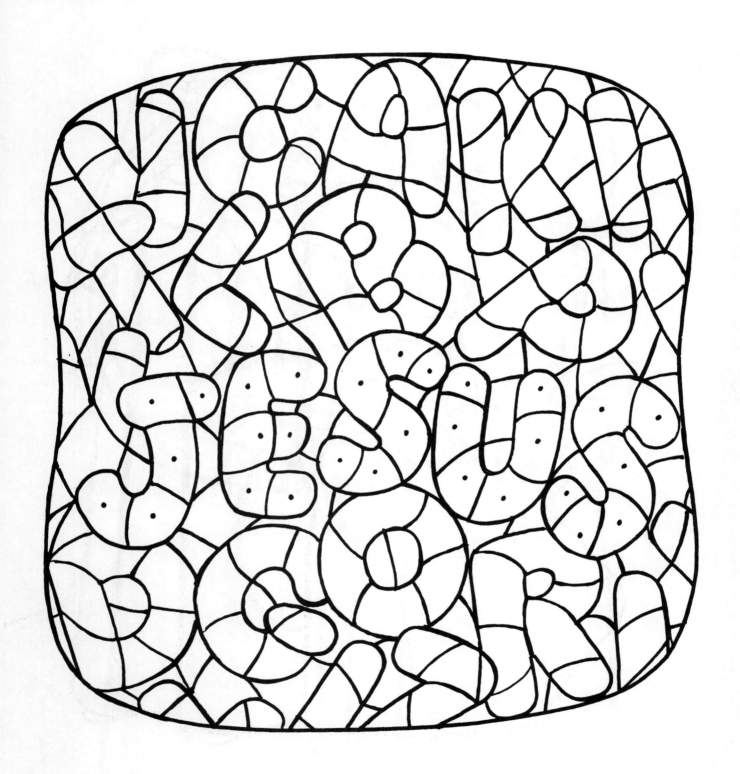

The Father has sent his Son to be the Savior of the world
1 John 4:14 NIV

Ruth and Naomi

Ruth was Naomi's daughter-in-law. Ruth loved Naomi and was very loyal to her, even though this meant Ruth left her home to live with Naomi. Because of this, God gave Ruth a wonderful husband and a baby boy.

Where you go I will go
Ruth 1:16 NIV

Loyalty means to be faithful and loving to someone, no matter what happens. We should be loyal to our parents, our friends, and our family just like Ruth was. Think of someone you can be loyal to. What can you do to show them you love them? Draw a picture of yourself being loyal to that person. Write your name on the blank line. Now give your picture to the person to show them you are loyal to them.

I will be loyal to you.

_____
(Your name)

A friend loves at all times
Proverbs 17:17

The Widow who gave

This widow was very poor. She and her son had only a little food left, but she gave all the food she had to Elijah, a great man of God. God provided food so the widow and her son were not hungry.

Give, and it will be given to you
Luke 6:38

God promises to us that when we give to others He will give us everything we need. Circle the things in the picture that you would give to someone who needed them. Then color the picture.

God loves a cheerful giver
2 Corinthians 9:7

Esther

Esther was a very kind and brave queen. When she heard that her people, the Jews, were going to be killed, Esther bravely risked her own life to save them from their enemy.

God is . . . a very present help in trouble
Psalm 46:1

God will help you to be brave and courageous just like Esther was. When you are afraid, God is with you to help you be brave. Circle the times when you would be afraid but God will give you courage.

Whenever I am afraid, I will trust in You.
Psalm 56:3

Mary and Martha

Mary and Martha were sisters. One day Jesus came to dinner. Martha was very busy cooking, while Mary sat and listened to Jesus. Jesus said Mary did the right thing by listening to Him first.

Seek first the kingdom of God
Matthew 6:33

Mary put Jesus first in her life. Look at each pair of pictures. Color the picture that shows someone who is putting Jesus first in their life.

Love the LORD your God with all your heart
Matthew 22:37

Dorcas

Dorcas was a kind, good woman. She made clothes for poor people. One day Dorcas died. The people she helped were sad. Peter prayed for her and she came back to life! The people were happy and many of them believed in Jesus.

Dorcas . . . was always doing good and helping the poor.
Acts 9:36 NIV

God wants us to be kind and helpful to each other. Draw a line from the picture on the left to the picture on the right that shows how you can be helpful.

Do not forget to do good and to share
Hebrews 13:16

Bible Boys and Girls

Joseph
Pages 51 and 52

Read or tell the Bible story from Genesis 37:3-4, 12-28 and Genesis 39-41.

Coloring Sheet: Read the picture caption to the children. Say, **God had a special plan for Joseph's life. He became a very important ruler in Egypt. God has a special plan for your life too. When we serve God, He will show us what He wants us to do.** Let the children tell what they would like to do when they grow up. Then say, **Whatever God wants us to do, it will be the very best thing for us. We must be willing to do whatever God wants us to do.** Talk about the memory verse and learn it as a class.

Activity Sheet: Review the events of Joseph's story as the children complete the maze. Say, **The Lord was with Joseph through all these events. When we serve the Lord, He is with us too.** Lead the children in saying aloud, "I want to serve the Lord. The Lord is with me," as they learn the memory verse.

Baby Moses
Pages 53 and 54

Read or tell the Bible story from Exodus 2:1-10 and Exodus 3:1-12.

Coloring Sheet: Ask the children to name things that they are afraid of or that might be dangerous. Ask them if they think God can protect them from these things. Say, **God protected Baby Moses from a cruel king who wanted to kill him. The Bible says God is with us and will watch over us.** Learn the memory verse together.

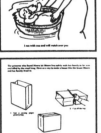

Activity Sheet: Let the children work together in pairs or groups to make Baby Moses' house out of grocery bags. (Smaller paper bags can be substituted for grocery bags, if desired.) The children may decorate their houses with markers if desired. As the children work, talk about God's protection of Moses. Then say, **The Bible says our helps comes from the Lord. God protected Baby Moses and God will protect us too.** Learn the verse as a class.

Samuel
Pages 55 and 56

Read or tell the Bible story from 1 Samuel 3:1-10, 19-21.

Coloring Sheet: Ask the class, **What would you do if you heard God talking to you? Would you listen and do what He said? That is what happened to Samuel.** Let the children talk about their reactions. Then say, **God had a very special job for Samuel to do, and God has special jobs for you to do too.** Talk about some of the things the children can do to serve the Lord. Learn the memory verse together. Then say, **God wants us to be listening for what He wants us to do.**

Activity Sheet: Say, **When God spoke to Samuel, Samuel could hear God's voice aloud. God usually does not speak aloud to people now, but He tells us what He wants us to do in other ways.** Talk about each of the pictures and decide if each is a way God speaks to people today. Ask, **Are you listening to hear what God is saying? Will you obey God when He tells you to do something?** Learn the memory verse together.

David
Pages 57 and 58

Read or tell the Bible story from 1 Samuel 17.

Coloring Sheet: Talk about the picture. Say, **How would you feel if you were going to battle against Goliath? David wasn't afraid because He knew God was with him. We can be unafraid too because God is with us also.** Learn the memory verse after discussing what it means to trust in the Lord. Talk about situations in which the children might be afraid, but instead they can trust in God.

Activity Sheet: Talk about Goliath's armor. Say, **Goliath believed his armor would protect him from David. David didn't wear any armor because God was protecting him. God's power is far greater than any armor or weapons.** Help the children to draw in what David and Goliath wore into battle. (The children may copy the picture on the Coloring Sheet.) Say, **When God is with us, we do not need to be afraid of anything, God's power is greater than any human power.** Learn the memory verse together as a class.

Jairus' daughter
Pages 59 and 60

Read or tell the Bible story from Mark 5:21-24, 35-43.

Coloring Sheet: Say, **Jesus has power over everything. Jesus can make sick people well and bring people who have died back to life.** Then ask, **Has Jesus ever made you well?** If you or someone you know has experienced a miraculous healing, share the story briefly. Then say, **Jesus gave us doctors and medicines to help make us well too. Sometimes doctors and medicines can't make us well. Jesus can.** Learn the memory verse.

Activity Sheet: Talk about the little girl who was brought back to life. Ask, **How do you think she felt? How would you feel if Jesus healed you? What would you do?** Let the children give their answers. Then say, **Jesus wants us to be thankful for His healing power.** Learn the memory verse and then help the children to connect the dots to show the little girl eating. Say, **God also wants us to take good care of our bodies. Jesus knew the little girl needed something good to eat to help her stay well.**

Timothy
Pages 61 and 62

Read or tell the story of Timothy from these selected verses: Acts 16:1-5, 1 Corinthians 4:17, 1 Corinthians 16:10, 2 Timothy 1:3-5.

Coloring Sheet: Talk about the ways Timothy helped Paul and Silas on their missionary trips. Then say, **Timothy learned about Jesus from his mother and grandmother when he was just a little boy. It is important that we learn about Jesus so we can serve Him too.** Let the children suggest ways they can serve the Lord now. Then say, **The Bible says people notice what a child does. You can share Jesus' love just by what you say and do.** Learn the memory verse.

Activity Sheet: Talk about ways the children can share Jesus' love by what they say and do. Then look at each picture and help the children decide if it shows an action which shares Jesus' loves with others. Let each child choose one way they will share Jesus' love this week. Learn the memory verse. Then say, **When we do what Jesus wants us to do, we are sharing the message of Jesus with other people like Timothy did.**

Joseph

Joseph's father gave Joseph a beautiful coat of many colors. Joseph's brothers sent Joseph to Egypt because they did not like him. But God was with Joseph and blessed him. This story teaches us that God has a wonderful plan for our lives.

All things work together for good to those who love God
Romans 8:28

Joseph went to visit his brothers who were with their sheep, but the brothers sent Joseph to Egypt. Find Joseph's path to visit his brothers and then on to Egypt.

The LORD was with Joseph
Genesis 39:2

Baby Moses

Moses' mother hid Moses in a basket so he would not be killed by the cruel king. Miraiam, Moses' sister, watched over him until God sent a **princess** to find him. Moses became a very important leader of God's people.

I am with you and will watch over you
Genesis 28:15 NIV

The princess who found Moses let Moses live safely with his family so he was not killed by the cruel king. Here is a way to make a house like the house Moses and his family lived in.

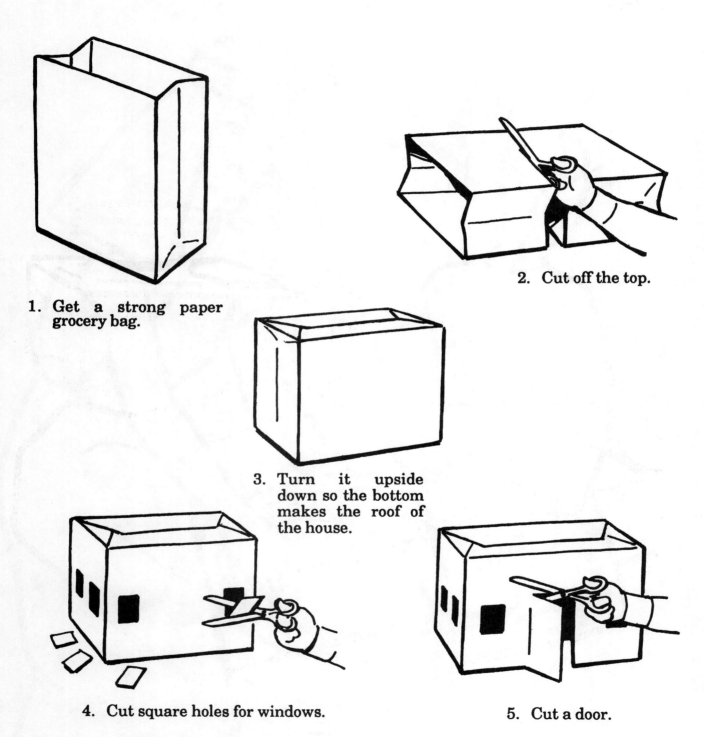

1. Get a strong paper grocery bag.

2. Cut off the top.

3. Turn it upside down so the bottom makes the roof of the house.

4. Cut square holes for windows.

5. Cut a door.

6. Now use your house to tell the story of Moses to someone else.

My help comes from the LORD
Psalm 121:2

Samuel

One night when Samuel was in bed, God told Samuel a special message about what He was going to do. Samuel became a good leader for God. This story teaches us that God has a special job for every boy and girl who will listen and obey God.

Speak (Lord), for your servant is listening
1 Samuel 3:10 NIV

God can speak to us in many ways. Circle the pictures that show some of these ways. Has God ever spoken to you? Are you listening to hear what God is saying?

I will hear what God the LORD will speak
Psalm 85:8

David

Goliath was a giant and an enemy of God's people. Goliath was dressed in heavy armor and carried a big spear, but David trusted in God, and killed Goliath with his slingshot.

I will trust and not be afraid
Isaiah 12:2

God helped David kill Goliath with only two things. Draw what David wore and carried into battle with Goliath. Then draw how Goliath was dressed for battle.

If God is for us, who can be against us?
Romans 8:31

Jairus' daughter

Jairus was a ruler of God's people. His little girl became sick and died, but Jesus brought her back to life again. This story teaches us that Jesus has power to heal people and bring the dead back to life.

I am the LORD who heals you.
Exodus 15:26

After Jesus brought Jairus' daughter back to life again, he told her parents to give her something. Connect the dots to see what Jesus wanted the little girl to do.

He commanded that she be given something to eat.
Luke 8:55

Timothy

Timothy went with Paul as a missionary. Paul and Timothy told many people about Jesus. Timothy went on special missionary trips by himself too. This story teaches us that even young people can tell others about Jesus.

Even a child is known by his actions
Proverbs 20:11 NIV

Boys and girls can tell the story of Jesus to others just like Timothy did. Circle the ways you can show the love of Jesus or tell someone else about Jesus. Cross out the actions that make Jesus sad.

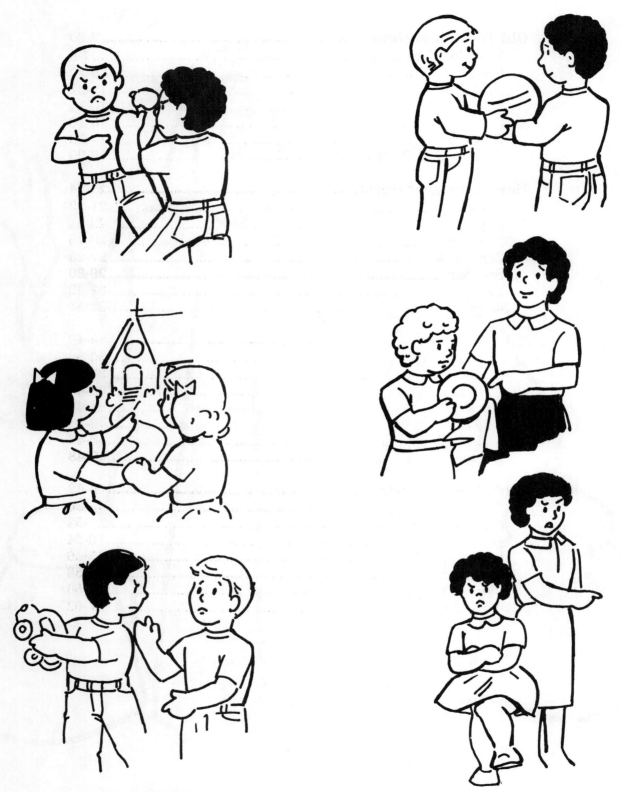

Go into all the world and preach the gospel
Mark 16:15

INDEX